THE WAY OF THE CROSS

The Way of the Cross

DONAGH O'SHEA, O.P.

DOMINICAN PUBLICATIONS

First published (2003) by
Dominican Publications
42 Parnell Square
Dublin 1

ISBN 1-871552-84-2

British Library Cataloguing in Publications Data.
A catalogue record for this book is available
from the British Library.

Illustrations: Maria Delia C. Zamora

Book and cover design by Bill Bolger.

Printed in Ireland by
The Leinster Leader Ltd, Naas, Co. Kildare

Acknowledgements
Scripture quotations are from the New Revised Standard Version
Bible copyright © 1989, by the Division of Christian Educationof
the National Council of Churches of Christ inthe USA, and are
used by permission. All rights reserved.

The English translation of the *Exultet* is from *Rite of Holy
Week* © 1972, International Committee on English in
the Liturgy. All rights reserved.

Contents

To look at the sun is not more difficult than to look at death. They are the opposite poles of our life: light and darkness. Death has been called 'the king of terrors'. We want to look away, but that will not help us. If we try to banish awareness of it, it will haunt us in terrible and gloomy shapes.

Christian awareness is shaped by a particular death: the death of Jesus. It is the death of one man, yes, but more; his disciples of every time and place are part of the picture. 'One has died for all; therefore all have died.' In a mysterious way we have died with him when we were baptised in his name. When we look at his death we see ours, and when we look at ours we see his. St Paul quoted an early Christian hymn, 'If we have died with him, we will also live with him.' His living and dying and rising are the energies that shape Christian identity.

From earliest times Christians have wanted to visit the Holy Land and see the places whose names were so familiar to them from the Scriptures. In following a path from the Praetorium to the house of Caiaphas and to Calvary they felt they were walking in the footsteps of Jesus, and identifying themselves spiritually with him.

When it became too difficult and even impossible to travel to the Holy Land, a custom arose in the sixteenth century (or possibly earlier) of creating at home a replica of Jesus' last journey. It would have been an outdoor way, with halting-places for prayer. Soon it was brought within the church building, and the stages marked by images on the wall. Today the fourteen 'Stations' are part of every Catholic church in the world.

There are many booklets in existence to help you 'do the Stations'. They differ greatly in tone, and this is useful because we are all different. Here, then, is another. Many people today are accustomed to add a fifteenth Station, the resurrection of Jesus. I have provided texts for this.

Part Two of this booklet is a resource for more leisurely reflection on each station. It provides scriptural texts, and it also brings us into the company of saints and mystics who have travelled this path before us.

On the road to Emmaus the two disciples failed to recognise the Risen Lord, and later they said, 'Were not our hearts burning within us while he was talking to us on the road?' This time may we recognise him, and may his very weakness give us strength to follow him who is 'the Way'.

O King of the Friday,
whose limbs were stretched on the cross,
O Lord who suffered the bruises, the pain, the loss,
we stretch ourselves
beneath the shield of your might;
may some fruit from the tree of your Passion
fall on us this night.

V. We adore you, O Christ, and we bless you,
R. Because by your holy cross you have redeemed the world.

Pilate, wishing to satisfy the crowd, released Barabbas for them;
and after flogging Jesus, he handed him over to be crucified.
(Mark 15:15)

'How lonely sits the city that once was full of people! How like a widow she has become!' Jesus is condemned to death. He is to be finally cut off from the people. Jerusalem, whose name means 'city of peace', is about to cut off the Prince of Peace. What will be left when he is dead? What will be the atmosphere of her streets tomorrow evening?

When I cut him off – when I cut anyone off, for we are all part of him – I choose a way of desolation, I disown the better part of myself. See my empty city, my withered heart, when I have passed judgment and washed my hands. See the unholy, see 'the dead land … the cactus land.' Pilate legalised the will of the crowd, 'Let him be crucified!' Hiding in the crowd was the faint-hearted Peter, who said merely, 'I never knew him!' We too, ever since, often by our lives, have repeated, 'I never knew him!'

Pause for silent prayer

Lord Jesus, our sin attempts to banish you from our lives. Your mercy is already manifest in the sublime silence and freedom with which you bore rejection. Give us grace to know what we are doing when we wash our hands among the guilty and settle into a false peace.

Lord, by your cross and resurrection
you have set us free.
You are the Saviour of the world.

V. We adore you, O Christ, and we bless you,
R. Because by your holy cross you have redeemed the world.

Carrying the cross by himself, Jesus went out to what is called The Place of the Skull, which in Hebrew is called Golgotha. (John 19:17)

The cross is laid on the shoulders of Jesus. He accepts it, because he has long since accepted it. Not many days before, he walked knowingly towards Jerusalem; the disciples ' were amazed, and those who followed were afraid.' He did not flee from suffering, but went towards it. He is not a victim but a hero. Therefore he lays no blame even on his executioners. Later his disciples would not be sparing with blame, but he blames no one. He allows himself to be led 'like a lamb that is led to the slaughter, and like a sheep that before its shearers is silent; so he did not open his mouth.'

He once told his disciples to take up their cross daily and follow him. He did not say, 'Take up *my* cross,' but 'Take up *your* cross.' Our crosses will not look like his, but it is through the grace of his cross that we discover the strength to carry ours.

Pause for silent prayer

Lord Jesus, you show us by your cross that love is stronger than death. In the immensity of your suffering we see the immensity of love. In the strength of your love for us may we take up the burden of the death of self. Give us the grace to carry our cross patiently, silently, lovingly, and at last even heroically.

Lord, by your cross and resurrection
you have set us free.
You are the Saviour of the world.

V. We adore you, O Christ, and we bless you,
R. Because by your holy cross you have redeemed the world.

Unless a grain of wheat falls into the earth and dies, it remains just a single grain; but if it dies, it bears much fruit. (John 12:24)

The gospels do not record that Jesus fell under the weight of the cross, but the fact that he had to be helped suggests it. He had already endured the ghastly Roman flogging, designed to take the victim to the brink of death. He came to the end of his strength, and then fell beyond it.

The 'Pantocrator' of Christian art, the 'All-Powerful One', lies prostrate on the earth. Had we never seen him in his weakness, he would not be like us in every way but sin. 'We do not have a high priest who is unable to sympathise with our weaknesses, but we have one who in every respect has been tested as we are, yet without sin.'

We know our own weaknesses very well, but perhaps not fully – because we have not been put fully to the test. Our oneness with him – the mysterious grace of our baptism in his name – is a promise that when we are pushed out beyond our limits we will meet him there.

Pause for silent prayer

Lord Jesus, you bore our sins in your body on the cross. When we discover further layers of sin and weakness in ourselves, may we take heart from your solidarity with us. When we fall may we know that it is by a miracle of grace that we are able to rise again, so that your grace may be manifest in our weakness.

Lord, by your cross and resurrection
you have set us free.
You are the Saviour of the world.

V. We adore you, O Christ, and we bless you,
R. Because by your holy cross you have redeemed the world.

Simeon said to his mother Mary, 'This child is destined for the falling and the rising of many in Israel, and to be a sign that will be opposed … and a sword will pierce your own soul too. (Luke 2:34-35)

For Mary also this was a road to Calvary. Simeon foretold it long ago, 'A sword shall pierce your own soul too.' The lance that pierced the side of Jesus pierced her too. That is the way with love. For a moment he entrusts his pain to her tenderness. Then they are separated by the jostling crowd and the soldiers intent on their duty. Human feelings are pushed aside; to a soldier's mind they are the sparks that could start a riot, and women have no business here in a man's world.

In our world, human feelings are easily pushed aside. They have no commercial value. The business world has its own urgencies and seldom stands back to let a human being pass. But what agonies we suffer in private! Public life is hard, and sometimes brutal; but why do we hide love from one another?

There, on the way to Calvary, in a vanishing moment, revealed only in a helpless gesture: the mystery of a fathomless love, 'the love that moves the sun and other stars.'

Pause for silent prayer

Lord Jesus, nothing had the power to deflect you from the way of love. Help us to accept that there is always pain when we try to love, and strengthen us to face it. May we feel the sorrows of others as our own and try to do all that their need may demand of us.

*Lord, by your cross and resurrection
you have set us free.
You are the Saviour of the world.*

FIFTH STATION – Simon of Cyrene Helps Jesus Carry His Cross

V. We adore you, O Christ, and we bless you,
R. Because by your holy cross you have redeemed the world.

They compelled a passer-by, who was coming in from the country, to carry his cross; it was Simon of Cyrene, the father of Alexander and Rufus. (Mark 15:21)

Simon is on his way home from work, looking forward to tomorrow, a free day. He is stopped by soldiers and ordered to help the prisoner on his way to execution. For the soldiers it is a matter of getting their work done, for Simon it is pressed service. There is no mention anywhere of pity or kindness. Afterwards Simon returns home, a little late; he turns his mind to other things, unaware that the incident will be remembered throughout the world and forever.

In God's providence we can do a kindness reluctantly or unawares, and our actions have meanings beyond our intention. The Son of God has placed himself humbly at our mercy, and stands in sore need even of grudging service. Even a feeble 'yes' is yes to the glory of God the Father, to the coming of his kingdom, to the accomplishment of his will on earth.

Pause for silent prayer

Lord Jesus, you are our deeper identity. You walked the path of humility with us, your brothers and sisters. Give us the good will to come to the aid of those who are weary and heavy-burdened. Take our reluctant service of one another and transform it into gracious deeds of kindness.

Lord, by your cross and resurrection
you have set us free.
You are the Saviour of the world.

SIXTH STATION – Veronica Wipes
the Face of Jesus

V. We adore you, O Christ, and we bless you,
R. Because by your holy cross you have redeemed the world.

He had no form or majesty that we should look at him, nothing
in his appearance that we should desire him. He was despised
and rejected by others … as one from whom others hide their
faces. (Isaiah 53:2-3)

Unlike Simon of Cyrene, Veronica is not mentioned in the
gospels. Unlike him too she comes forward voluntarily to offer
kindness to Jesus. She steps out from 'the women who were
beating their breasts and wailing for him', or perhaps she steps
out of the imagination of countless Christians through the ages
who wished they had been there to do what she did. She has a
good heart and she is moderately heroic. She represents ordinary kindness, a form of love within the reach of everyone.

'Christ's humanity is the true Adam.' He is every man and
woman; he is our deeper identity. He is the one showing
kindness, and also the one in need of it. On our road to Calvary
we meet him every day, almost every hour. A thousand faces are
in need of the 'little, nameless, unremembered acts of kindness,'
and they will leave in our spirit the imprint of his features.

Pause for silent prayer

Lord Jesus, in your person all humanity is formed into a unity
and bound to God; you are the face of all humanity. Give us
eyes to see you suffering in our suffering brothers and sisters.
May be never refuse them ordinary kindness, may we never
ignore the most trivial duty of neighbourliness, or the most
diffident plea for help.

Lord, by your cross and resurrection
you have set us free.
You are the Saviour of the world.

V. We adore you, O Christ, and we bless you,
R. Because by your holy cross you have redeemed the world.

Jesus said to them, 'I am deeply grieved, even to death ....' And going a little further, he threw himself on the ground and prayed that, if it were possible, the hour might pass from him. (Mark 14:34-35)

He who is 'the reflection of God's glory and the exact imprint of God's very being', joined himself to us, taking on the awesome burden of humanity. The sinless one placed himself at the mercy of a humanity that is soiled and mutilated in us. He is 'a lamp shining in a dark place,' and the darkness takes its vengeance. We see him fall to the ground under the burden. 'He bore our sins in his body'.

The word 'success' does not occur in the gospels, and the word 'victory' occurs there only in quotation from the Old Testament. To all appearances Jesus' life was a complete failure. Even his death seems a failure: he is too weak to walk proudly to the scaffold as the heroes of history-books do. He is human beyond words. He weakens, stumbles and falls. In one and the same moment we glimpse the vast humility of love and the hollow heart of success.

Pause for silent prayer

Lord Jesus, you humbled yourself even to death on a cross. Teach us to recognise you in the prostrate figures of the sick, the poor, the homeless, the rejected. And when we ourselves begin to weaken, and failure presses heavily on us, and we learn the taste of desolation, may we find hope through the incorruptibility of your love.

Lord, by your cross and resurrection
you have set us free.
You are the Saviour of the world.

EIGHTH STATION – Jesus Speaks to the Women of Jerusalem

V. We adore you, O Christ, and we bless you,
R. Because by your holy cross you have redeemed the world.

A great number of the people followed him, and among them were women who were beating their breasts and wailing for him. But Jesus turned to them and said, 'Daughters of Jerusalem, do not weep for me, but weep for yourselves and for your children.' (Luke 23:27-28)

In Jerusalem it was a custom for women to offer drinks to condemned criminals on their way to death. Women know how to stay close to suffering. They are weeping for him, and he speaks to them. Weep for worse to come, he says, foreseeing the terrible destruction of the city by the Romans and the scattering of the nation. 'Do not weep for me.' Even in the extremity of pain he is able to feel for others. He is still weeping for Jerusalem.

It was the religious authorities in Jerusalem who compassed his death; it was the citizens of Jerusalem who swayed Pilate's judgment against him when they raised the cry, 'Crucify him!' Still he weeps for Jerusalem. The corruption of the Temple cult and the clergy's exploitation of the poor moved him to anger, as did the heartlessness of their teaching. And still he weeps for Jerusalem.

He was angry with them, because he could not be indifferent to the oppressed; he could weep with sorrow; but he could not hate.

Pause for silent prayer

Lord Jesus, your enemies attempted to destroy you, but could not destroy your capacity to love. May we not be embittered by suffering; may it keep our hearts open even to our enemies; may it deepen and strengthen us to love.

Lord, by your cross and resurrection
you have set us free.
You are the Saviour of the world.

V. We adore you, O Christ, and we bless you,
R. Because by your holy cross you have redeemed the world.

'Come to me, all who that are weary and are carrying heavy burdens, and I will give you rest. Take my yoke upon you and learn from me; for I am gentle and humble in heart, and you will find rest for your souls.' (Matthew 11:28-29)

Christian devotion sees Jesus fall a third time under the weight of the cross. Why three times? Why do we need to contemplate this painful moment repeatedly? It is because we need to know him near us not only when we fall once or twice, but in our prolonged and growing weakness. His journey to Calvary is our journey through life, into the heart of the Paschal mystery. Though a young man, he experiences our long road, the closing-in of horizons, the fated ebb-tide of our powers.

The one who gave strength to others, who said to the crippled man, 'Take up your mat and walk,' is unable to stand or move. He is mysteriously in need of our help. Every instinct in us rises up to help him. We feel the need to give to him, and not only to receive. He gives himself completely: he has not given us everything until he has given us his capacity to give. We lift him up when we lift up the least of his brothers or sisters.

Pause for silent prayer

Lord Jesus, you did not abandon us in our weakness, but you became wretched and weak for our sake, to save us from the deeper wretchedness of despair. Be with us when we grow weary in our illness, when the road seems too long, and we are humbled by our dependence on others. May the grace of your humility raise up our spirit.

Lord, by your cross and resurrection
you have set us free.
You are the Saviour of the world.

TENTH STATION – Jesus Is Stripped of His Garments

V. We adore you, O Christ, and we bless you,
R. Because by your holy cross you have redeemed the world.

They divided his clothes among them, casting lots to decide what each should take. (Mark 15:24)

The man who had 'nowhere to lay his head' is now stripped of his garments. It is impossible to be poorer than this. He stands before the Father 'in Adam's tunic,' his wounded human flesh. He is suffering all the consequences of having taken on himself the sins and shame of the old Adam. Only the eyes of faith – and that with hindsight – could see in this trembling, defenceless man the new Adam, the new human being, the best of what we are to be. Standing at the place of execution, he is the very image of humiliation and defeat; but the eye of faith sees in him 'the image of the invisible God, the first-born of all creation'.

'Life does not consist in the abundance of possessions,' he once said. 'Life is more than food, and the body more than clothing.' Now he shows, without words, that there is a reality even deeper than the life of the body: 'blessed are the poor in spirit'. He reaches further and further in, deeper and deeper: clothing, body, spirit. Layer by layer, Adam (that is, the whole Christ, head and members) is stripped down till the spirit rings with integrity and can hear the Father's voice, 'You are my Son, the Beloved'.

Pause for silent prayer

Lord Jesus, in you the deepest mystery of humanity is laid bare in all its vulnerability. Help us, as far as we are able to endure it, to know ourselves as we are in your sight. Seeing our hearts in the light of your holiness may we put away everything that distracts us from the path of love.

> Lord, by your cross and resurrection
> you have set us free.
> You are the Saviour of the world.

ELEVENTH STATION – Jesus Is Nailed
to the Cross

V. We adore you, O Christ, and we bless you,
R. Because by your holy cross you have redeemed the world.

It was nine o'clock in the morning when they crucified him. The inscription of the charge against him read, 'The King of the Jews'. And with him they crucified two bandits, one on his right and one on his left. (Mark 15:25-27)

Jesus said to the man with the withered hand, 'Stretch out your hand,' and he was healed. To another, who was unable to walk, he said, 'Stand up, take your mat and walk,' and at once the man began to walk. Our hands are our power to do things, our feet are our power to go where we will. Now he stretches out his own limbs, not for healing but for death. 'I came not to judge the world,' he said, but the world judges him and finds him unworthy to live among us. 'I came that they may have life,' he said, but he is repaid with death.

'Father, forgive them, for they do not know what they are doing.' How could they or anyone know? They were not crucifying a criminal but 'the Lord of glory'; they were not cutting him off but binding him forever to the heart of the world; they were not ending his life but releasing through him a flood of new life that no power on earth could destroy.

Pause for silent prayer

Lord Jesus, you joined yourself to us in a bond that death could not break but only strengthen. When sickness and problems hold us in their grip, may we find wisdom and strength to endure through the mystery of your cross.

Lord, by your cross and resurrection
you have set us free.
You are the Saviour of the world.

V. We adore you, O Christ, and we bless you,
R. Because by your holy cross you have redeemed the world.

When it was noon, darkness over the whole land until three in the afternoon. At three o'clock Jesus cried out with a loud voice, 'Eloi, Eloi, lema sabachthani?' which means, 'My God, my God, why have you forsaken me?' … Then Jesus gave a loud cry and breathed his last. (Mark 15:33-39)

The cross is raised between heaven and earth. Jesus is rejected by humanity and abandoned by his Father. He has pierced through to the very heart of pain and loneliness. In that frightful void, hope will be reborn for a lost world. 'My God, my God, why have you forsaken me?' His words are the cry of all humanity; in his mouth they are words of redemption. He is redeeming all humanity who from that day till now have abandoned God or felt abandoned by God. He is redeeming atheists and agnostics, and all the bereaved of all time and place, the depressed, the abandoned, the mentally ill … all who have ever been visited by the dark angel of suffering.

Death silences even those who stand watching. We have heard the words of Jesus, we must also hear his silence. We have to sit with pain and sorrow and resist the temptation to 'solve' them or avoid them. Only into silence will they pour out their meaning.

Pause for silent prayer

Lord Jesus, you have gone before us into death and discovered there the Father's loving will. You breathed your last in agony, but your next breath was the Holy Spirit you breathed on the disciples at Easter. Through the grace of your Resurrection may we discover faith when we are defeated, hope when all is dark, and love hiding in the heart of pain.

*Lord, by your cross and resurrection
you have set us free.
You are the Saviour of the world.*

V. We adore you, O Christ, and we bless you,
R. Because by your holy cross you have redeemed the world.

When [the soldiers] came to Jesus and saw that he was already
dead, they did not break his legs. Instead, one of the soldiers
pierced his side with a spear, and at once blood and water came
out. (John 19:32-34)

Mary receives the dead body of her Son. The mind is drawn
back to Bethlehem: the cycle of pain is complete, the Mother-
and-Child scene is now the *Pietà*. It was to this that she said her
trusting 'yes' at the Annunciation, though she could not have
known. 'Unless a grain of wheat falls into the earth and dies, it
remains just a single grain; but if it dies, it bears much fruit.'
Mary is addressed as 'Earth' in the Byzantine liturgy: 'Blessed
Earth, blissful spouse of God, who made the unsown Wheat to
grow, the Saviour of the world ....'

Mary is the perfect disciple, fully united with the work of
redemption. She is the first sign that his sacrifice was not in
vain. She is called 'Mother of the Church'. To share in her
fecundity the Church has to retain her maternal qualities: her
tender love, her pondering of the word, her humility. The self-
effacement of love is personalised in her. 'This is how we should
be,' wrote a saint, 'nothing to show on the outside, nothing to
impress the eyes of the world ... all the splendour is within.'

Pause for silent prayer

Lord Jesus, you loved us to the end; you gave us the gift of your
humanity till there was no more to give. Give us also the grace
to receive your gift, and to live the new life of love that you have
made possible for us. Give us strength to embrace our suffering,
and not to part from it till it has accomplished your purpose in
us.

Lord, by your cross and resurrection
you have set us free.
You are the Saviour of the world.

FOURTEEENTH STATION – Jesus Is Laid in the Tomb

V. We adore you, O Christ, and we bless you,
R. Because by your holy cross you have redeemed the world.

When [Pilate] learned from the centurion that [Jesus] was dead,
he granted the body to Joseph. Then Joseph bought a linen cloth,
and taking down the body, wrapped it in the linen cloth, and
laid it in a tomb which had been hewn out of the rock. He then
rolled a stone against the door of the tomb. (Mark 15:45-47)

St Paul is at pains to say that Jesus not only died but was buried.
Burial is the completion of death, the evidence of its reality:
Jesus not only died but was swallowed up in death. We are not
allowed to let the resurrection make his death incomplete or less
real. 'I handed on to you as of first importance what I in turn
had received,' St Paul wrote, 'that Christ died for our sins …
and that he was buried … ' The stone rolled against the entrance
to the tomb is proof that everything that happened before is
definitively in the past.

The Church does not celebrate the Eucharist on Good Friday.
The altars are stripped bare, the whole Church is one with
Christ in his death. We have to look at what power does to love;
the Christian heart feels the darkness of the world, and allows
itself to look at the darkness itself.

Pause for silent prayer

Lord Jesus, so complete was the Incarnation that you experienced every stage of our life and death. May we not squander
the precious gift of life, nor grieve over death as those who have
no hope. May the sadness of death give way to the bright
promise of eternal life.

> *Lord, by your cross and resurrection*
> *you have set us free.*
> *You are the Saviour of the world.*

FIFTEENTH STATION – Jesus Is Raised from the Dead

V. We adore you, O Christ, and we bless you,
R. Because by your holy cross you have redeemed the world.

'Why do you look for the living among the dead? He is not here, but has risen.' (Luke 24:5)

The Resurrection of Jesus from the dead is God's most triumphal deed, and the corner-stone of our faith. Evil has not been victorious: from the worst that human beings can do comes a victory beyond our imagining. It is Easter Sunday that makes Good Friday good. It is the end that gives meaning to the story.

In the darkness we rise for the Easter Vigil. Against a black sky we light the Easter fire. But this would be a forlorn gesture if Christ were not risen from the dead! Suddenly the Paschal candle is alight. *Lumen Christi!* – the light of Christ lightens our darkness. *Exsultet!* – 'Exult, all creation … ! Rejoice, O earth, in shining splendour, radiant in the brightness of your King …. Darkness vanishes forever … ! Let this place resound with joy, echoing the mighty song of all God's people!'

Pause for silent prayer

Lord Jesus, in you a new age has dawned, the long reign of sin is ended, a broken world has been renewed, and we are once again made whole. You have made us children of the light, rising to new and eternal life. We praise you for the joy of the resurrection that fills the whole world.

Lord, by your cross and resurrection
you have set us free.
You are the Saviour of the world.

This section provides resources for further reflection and prayer at each Station. Sometimes one may want to sit at each Station (or at a particular one) rather than stay on the move. The very word 'station' means a stopping-place – the opposite of 'way'! If you are experiencing a special difficulty in your life, it may be helpful to do the Stations at this slower rate – perhaps one each day, or just a particular one.

Jesus Is Condemned to Death

Luke 23:20-25

Pilate, wanting to release Jesus, addressed them; again; but they kept shouting, 'Crucify, crucify him!' A third time he said to them, 'Why, what evil has he done? I have found in him no ground for the sentence of death; I will therefore have him flogged and then release him.' But they kept urgently demanding with loud shouts that he should be crucified; and their voices prevailed. So Pilate gave his verdict that their demand should be granted. He released the man they asked for, the one who had been put in prison for insurrection and murder, and he handed Jesus over as they wished.

John 19:1-3

Pilate took Jesus and had him flogged. And the soldiers wove a crown of thorns and put it on his head, and they dressed him in a purple robe. They kept coming up to him, saying, 'Hail, King of the Jews!' and striking him on the face.

To condemn the great is to condemn oneself to their absence. 'Do not judge, so that you may not be judged,' Jesus once said. Pilate passed judgment on himself and on the crowd whose will he followed. If I evict Jesus from my life, or if I allow him only a limited place in it, I am evicting myself from my inheritance. A fifth-century Syrian monk, Dionysius the Areopagite, expressed this graphically.

> If you are standing in a boat and you try to push away a rock that is in your way, that will not affect the rock, which stands immovable, but will distance you from it; and the more you push, the more you are distanced .... Similarly, if you pull on a rope that is attached to the rock, you would not draw the rock towards you, but you would draw yourself and your boat towards the rock.

The image clarifies one aspect of the truth, but obscures another. We can push ourselves away from God and Christ, but it is *grace* that draws us, not our own effort. 'No one can come to me unless *drawn by the Father*' (John 6:44). St Augustine commented on this verse:

> Do not suppose here any rough and uneasy violence. It is gentle; it is sweet; it is the very sweetness that draws you. Is not a sheep drawn when fresh grass is shown to it in its hunger. Yet I imagine that it is not driven bodily on, but bound by desire. In this way too you come to Christ: do not imagine a long journey; in the very place where you believe, there you come. For to him who is everywhere we come by love, but by sailing. But since even in this kind of voyage waves and tempests and different temptations abound, believe in the Crucified so that your faith may be able to mount the Cross. You will not sink; you will be borne on the wood of the Cross. It was in this way that he sailed amid the waves of this world, the one who said, 'God forbid that I

should glory save in the Cross of our Lord Jesus Christ'
(Galatians 6:14).

The attractive power of Jesus in his suffering lies in this. Unlike the destructive heroes of the cinema he does not destroy his enemies, but wins them with love. To watch the death of Jesus is certainly to watch a horrible event, but its meaning lies in the way he transformed the world of tribunals, judgment, torture, and sentence of death into something of infinite depth. To follow the Way of the Cross is to contemplate this mystery.

Jesus Takes up
His Cross

Isaiah 53:5-7

He was wounded for our transgressions, crushed for our iniquities; upon him was the punishment that made us whole, and by his bruises we are healed. All we like sheep have gone astray; we have all turned to our own way, and the Lord has laid on him with the iniquity of us all. He was oppressed and he was afflicted, yet he did not open his mouth; like a sheep that is led to the slaughter, and like a sheep that before its shearers is silent, so he did not open his mouth.

Mark 15:20

After mocking him, they stripped him of the purple cloak and put his own clothes on him. Then they led him out to crucify him.

Luke 9:23

Then he said to them all, 'If any want to become my followers, let them deny themselves and take up their cross daily and follow me.'

Watch this procession: 'They were on the road, going up to

Jerusalem, and Jesus was walking ahead of them; they were amazed, and those who followed were afraid.' He and everyone else knew that he was walking to his death. It is normal to avoid suffering, but he was going straight towards it.

We are being shown that it is wiser to face suffering than to flee from it. If I always flee from suffering, it will catch up with me anyway, and then I will be a victim. But if I go towards it, then even if it defeats me I will be a hero. Jesus was a hero, not a victim. It is true that because of the metaphor of Paschal Lamb he has been called 'victim' (though not in the New Testament), but this was meant in a ritual, not a psychological sense; it does not sanctify a false kind of passivity, a 'victim mentality'. In the psychological sense. The word 'victim' entails a whole family of words, some of which have no place in the spiritual search: aggressor, injustice, pleading, blaming, complaining …. We also have to look carefully at the things it has led people to say about God the Father – for example, in a nineteenth century hymn:

> All Heaven's Wrath though due to us
> On him, our Victim, lay.

The 'wrath' of God is another member of the family. Christ, our Paschal Lamb, walked towards suffering and death, and refused to blame anyone for it. A passive psychology would have led him to run in the opposite direction.

Suffering is our best teacher. It pierces the illusions of the ego and brings us into direct contact with reality. It would be a

shame to destroy that effect by weaving further illusions around
suffering itself.

Julian of Norwich, the fourteenth-century English mystic, had a vigorous and realistic attitude to suffering, and to life in general. She wrote:

> Jesus said … with complete confidence, 'You will not be overcome.' All this teaching, with its true encouragement, applies to all my fellow-Christians … and it is God's will. These words, 'You will not be overcome', were said very insistently and emphatically to give me confidence and strength for every trouble that may come. He did not say 'You will not have a hard time; you will not be burdened; you will not have to face difficulties.' He said, 'You will not be overcome.' God wants us to pay attention to these words so that we can always be strong and confident, through good and bad times. God loves us and delights in us, so he wants us to love and delight in him and trust him implicitly. So all will be well.

Jesus Falls
the First Time

Isaiah 53:6-8

All we like sheep have gone astray; we have all turned to our own way, and the Lord has laid on him with the iniquity of us all. He was oppressed and he was afflicted, yet he did not open his mouth; like a sheep that is led to the slaughter, and like a sheep that before its shearers is silent, so he did not open his mouth. By a perversion of justice he was taken away. Who could have imagined his future ? For he was cut off from the land of the living, stricken for the transgression of my people.

Psalm 37

O Lord, your hand has come down upon me.…
I am utterly bowed down and prostrate.…
My heart throbs, my strength fails me;
as for the light of my eyes – it also has gone from me.
My friends and companions stand aloof from my affliction,
and my neighbours stand afar off.

The central image in Julian of Norwich's *Shewings* is that of a Lord and servant. The servant stands before his Lord, ready to leap up and run to do his will. But as soon as he moves he falls into a deep pit and is severely wounded. The Lord, as we may expect, is God; but notice while you read this passage who, in succession, the figure of the servant represents.

> Filled with wonder, I gazed at the Lord and the servant ….
> There were two ways of looking at the servant – one
> outward, the other inward. Outwardly, he was dressed
> simply, like a workman ready to do his work, and he stood
> very near his Lord …. He was wearing a single white tunic,
> old and shapeless, stained, marked by sweat, tight and short,
> coming barely below the knee. It was threadbare – almost
> worn out – and looked as if it was about to fall to pieces ….

> The servant stands for the second person of the Trinity and
> also for Adam, that is, humankind. When I say the Son, that
> means Christ in his divinity, equal with the Father, and
> when I say the servant, that means Christ's humanity, which
> is the true Adam …. The Lord is God the Father, the servant
> is the Son, Jesus Christ, and the Holy Spirit is the love which
> is in them both equally.

> When Adam (that is, all humankind) fell, God's Son fell ….
> Adam fell from life to death, into the depths of this wretched
> world, and then into hell. God's Son fell, with Adam, into
> the depths of the virgin's womb – herself the fairest daughter
> of Adam – in order to let Adam off from all blame in heaven
> and on earth. Then, with wonderful power he drew Adam
> out of hell.

> The wisdom and the goodness which were in the servant
> point to God's Son. The workman's shabby clothes …
> represent Jesus' humanity and also Adam, with all the

ensuing trouble and weakness. Throughout all this our good Lord revealed his Son and Adam as only one man. Our virtue and goodness are from Jesus Christ, our weakness and blindness from Adam. Both could be seen in that one servant.

Thus our good Lord Jesus has taken upon himself all our blame, and our Father may not, and does not intend, to blame us any more than he blamed his dear Son.

Jesus Meets His Mother

Lamentations 1:12

Is it nothing to you, all you who pass by?
Look and see if there is any sorrow like
my sorrow, which was brought upon me.

Luke 2:34-35

Simeon blessed them and said to his mother Mary, 'This child
is destined for the falling and the rising of many in Israel, and
to be a sign that will be opposed so that the inner thoughts of
many will be revealed – and a sword will pierce your own soul
too.'

✠

The gospels do not record this meeting of Jesus and his mother,
but since John's gospel places her beside the cross, it is reason-
able to picture their meeting on the way. Traditional piety
forebears to put words in their mouths. This was a good
instinct. Their language was silence. Or rather, revealed by the
silence, *presence*. Physical presence is our first language in every
sense: as infants we were in the world some time before we
began to speak ('*in-fantes*': non-speakers); and throughout our
lives *presence* continues to be more profound than speech,
which is our second language. We learn that first language from

our mothers, as later on we begin to learn the second. It was appropriate that Jesus and his mother should communicate in the deepest language at that moment.

Silence is also the language of contemplation. In contemplation all story-telling, however good and edifying, has to stop. Spoken language opens the spirit, but only so far. Grammar and logic are the hoops around my barrel: they are always holding a particular version of the world together. To be more deeply receptive to God I must fall silent.

Ignatius of Antioch was sent as a prisoner to Rome during the reign of the Emperor Trajan (A.D. 98 – 117) to face martyrdom. Along the way he wrote seven letters to various communities of Christians. The following passage is from one of them.

> Indeed, it is better to keep quiet and *be*, than to make fluent professions and *not be*. No doubt it is a fine thing to instruct others, but only if the speakers practise what they preach. One such Teacher there is: the One who 'spoke and it was made;' and what he achieved even by his silences was well worthy of the Father. Those who have truly mastered the utterances of Jesus will also be able to apprehend his silence, and thus reach full spiritual maturity, so that their own words have the force of actions and their silences the significance of speech.

Simon of Cyrene Helps Jesus Carry His Cross

Mark 15:21
They compelled a passer-by, who was coming in from the country, to carry his cross: Simon of Cyrene, the father of Alexander and Rufus.

Galatians 6:1-2
If anyone is detected in a transgression, you who have received the Spirit should restore such a one in a spirit of gentleness. Take care that you yourselves are not tempted. Bear one another's burdens, and in this way you will fulfil the law of Christ.

Simon is the model of all involuntary workers. We have much to learn from him – more, it may be, than from more perfect people. Many people dislike their work and would give it up without regret if they could afford to do so. This may be a more general condition today, but it is not new. Hear from someone who lived about 2,500 years ago:

> Do not human beings have a hard service on earth,
> and are not our days like the days of a labourer?
> Like the slave who longs for the shadow,
> and like labourers who look for their wages ….

Our age has been called the age of *alienation*. To be alienated is to feel an outsider to what is happening; but more deeply it is to feel an outsider to oneself. Many people today feel lonely and disconnected, despite the almost miraculous new technologies of communication. Our need is deeper than the need to *know*; we need to feel *involved,* heart and soul, in what is going on around us and in us. The mind's instinct is to *analyse* – a word whose Greek origin means 'to undo, to loosen'. We need putting back together again.

What is my gut feeling about the human world around me? Am I part of it or not? Am I 'in it but not of it'? Can I be *one with it*, damaged and all as it is, damaged and all as I am? And the natural world: can I be *one with it*? To put it another way, Can I love it? Can I welcome its laws and find them not alien to me? And can I seriously love God? Can I be *one with* God? Does the 'law of God' feel alien to me and threatening? What if I realise that the law of God is *love*?

Gregory the Great (A.D. c. 540 – 604) wrote:

> What should the 'law' of God be taken to mean, if not love? By love we learn inwardly how the commandments of life are to be put into practice. Concerning this law the voice of Truth has said, 'This is my commandment, that you love lone another.' Concerning it Paul says, 'Love is the fulfilling of the law.' Again, he says 'Bear one another's burdens, and so fulfil the law of Christ.' What can the law of Christ be more rightly understood to mean, than love? And we truly fulfil his law when, for the sake of love, we bear the burdens of others.

Henry Suso (c. 1300 – 1366), a disciple of Meister Eckhart, had
to take account of a movement called 'The Brethren of the Free
Spirit'. These proclaimed that the true believer was bound by
no law. In the following passage Suso *deepens* and *interiorises* the
notion of law.

> '*Question*: St Paul says that no law is made for the just. ('The
> law is laid down not for the just but for the lawless and
> disobedient' 1 Timothy 1:9).
>
> *Answer:* The just, insofar as they are just, conduct themselves
> more submissively than other people because they under-
> stand *from within in the ground of their being* what is proper
> outwardly, and they view all things accordingly. The reason
> that they are not fettered is that they themselves do *freely* out
> of an attitude of detachment what ordinary people do under
> compulsion.'

A monk once asked a Zen master if the enlightened person was
subject to the law of cause-and-effect. Yes sounds like slavery,
and No sounds like anarchy. The answer was neither Yes nor
No. There is a middle way, or rather a way that is deeper than
both. 'The enlightened person is *one with* the law of cause-and-
effect.' 'To be one with' a law is to have interiorised it. It is no
longer an imposed law. 'To be one with' is another way of
saying love.

Many of the mystics are teaching us this lesson, which was
natural to people of other times and places, but which may seem
new to us. Here is a passage from Meister Eckhart (1260 – 1328):

> [Jesus said] 'This is my *commandment* [that you love one

another] ....' When I am thirsty, the drink commands me; when I am hungry, the food commands me. And God does the same. He commands me to such sweetness that the whole world cannot equal. And if people have once tasted this sweetness, then indeed they can no more turn away with their love from goodness and from God, than God can turn away from His Godhead.

Veronica Wipes the Face of Jesus

Isaiah 52:14

Just as there were many who were aston-
ished at him – so marred was his appearance, beyond human semblance, and his
form beyond that of mortals – so shall he
startle many nations, kings shall shut
their mouths because of him; for that which had not been told
them they shall see, and that which they had not heard they shall
contemplate.

Philippians 2:6-7

Though he was in the form of God, [Jesus] did not regard
equality with God as something to be exploited, but emptied
himself, taking the form of a slave, being born in human
likeness. And being found in human form, he humbled himself
and became obedient to the point of death – even death on a
cross.

To wipe someone's face is an intimate service; it is in the order
of things that mothers do for their children. Veronica's gesture
shows the advanced frailty of Jesus. Only that – and love –
entitles you to wipe another's face. Normally we stay a little

further back from people; we don't focus straight into the detail of their presence. With strangers we are inclined to stay well back and choose a topic that is literally as broad as the sky: the weather. Veronica moves into the zone of intimacy and wipes the face of Jesus. He leaves the imprint of his pain and distress on the cloth. There is nothing 'general' anywhere to be seen; everything there is full of particularity.

Everything in the world is particular. There is no such reality as people in general, or pain in general, or love in general. There aren't even trees in general, or birds in general. In this poem G.M. Hopkins celebrates the particularity of everything: a flash of colour in the movement of a bird, a sound ….

> As kingfishers catch fire, dragonflies dráw fláme;
> As tumbled over rim in roundy wells
> Stones ring; like each tucked string tells, each hung bell's
> Bow swung finds tongue to fling out broad its name;
> Each mortal thing does one thing and the same:
> Deals out that being indoors each one dwells;
> Selves—goes itself; *myself* it speaks and spells,
> Crying *Whát I do is me: for that I came.*
>
> Í say móre: the just man justices;
> Kéeps gráce: thát keeps all his goings graces;
> Acts in God's eye what in God's eye he is—
> Chríst—for Christ plays in ten thousand places,
> Lovely in limbs, and lovely in eyes not his
> To the Father through the features of men's faces.

'Christ plays in ten thousand places,' yet he is not an abstraction

or a 'generality': he is really touched and met in all his
particularity in each person; every person is a kind of sacramental presence of Christ. He is 'lovely in eyes not his,' and yet they are his; they are not just reminders of him. In God's eyes every person is Christ. If we can see another person in God we see him or her as Christ. 'Jesus is all who shall be saved, and all who shall be saved are Jesus,' wrote Julian of Norwich.

The blood, sweat, and tears on the face of every child of Adam are the imprint of the features of Jesus. Veronica met pain with compassion, and that is the most fundamental process of our life.

A final offering: lines from Rabindranath Tagore:

> The day was when I did not keep myself in readiness for Thee; and entering my heart unbidden even as one of the common crowd, unknown to me, my King, Thou didst press the signet of eternity upon many a fleeting moment of my life.

Jesus Falls
a Second Time

Psalm 37

For I am ready to fall,
and my pain is ever with me.

Psalm 68

Save me O God,
for the waters have come up to my neck.
I sink in deep mire,
where there is no foothold;
I have come into deep waters,
and the flood sweeps over me.
I am weary with my crying,
my throat is parched.
My eyes grow dim ….

Hebrews 5:8

Although he was a Son, he learned obedience through what he suffered.

We would like to be winners, not heroes. Winning means competing successfully, being better than others. This of course is small comfort unless others know about it. If there is no applause I scarcely exist, but when there is applause I am still not happy: I am gripped with fear that it will fade, because when it fades I fade. Thus everything is driven by the fear of failure. Competitive people appear outer-directed and other-directed: they give the impression of having an out-going personality. But fear is not an out-going instinct; quite the contrary.

Jesus was often in conflict with the religious authorities, but he was never in competition with them: he was not looking for what they had. He did not compete with the powerful, he empowered the powerless. Your arm is your power to do things; he restored the use of his arm to the man with 'the withered hand.' Your feet are your power to go places; he healed the crippled man at the pool. He even populated his stories with powerless people: 'Go out at once into the streets and lanes of the town and bring in the poor, the crippled, the blind, and the lame.'

Now he is weak himself; his legs will no longer support him, and he falls. It is not like the fall of a winner. A winner's fall is from a height, but Jesus was already among the lowest and weakest people. His fall gives him an even closer identification with them; it is a kind of homecoming. For a winner it would be exile.

When I try to help the poor, the powerless, the anxious, I must locate their qualities in myself. If I don't, I may be subtly competing with the very people I am attempting to help: I may be secretly rejoicing in the difference between me and them. Then I will have a hidden interest in keeping them the way they are. Their recovery would threaten my position as helper. I *fear* they may be helped.

Here is a passage from the Sufi mystic, Jelaluddin Rumi (1207
– 1273).

You have been imitating spirituality.
Imitation is a lock in your chest.
Dissolve it with tears … !

Imitation

is a blind man describing a landscape
with beautiful words.
There's no heart-knowledge.
The blind man gets excited with the words,
but you feel the distance between him and the beauty ….
The imitator is a professional mourner,
with no motive but money.
The words burn, but there's no warmth,
and no broken-open-ness ….
Though even the imitator gets some reward,
as professional mourners get their wages ….
The difference between being with a true knower
and being with an imitator
is like the difference between
being in the presence of the prophet David
and being outside somewhere,
hearing a vague echo sound:
David is a source. The imitator
has just memorised a few psalms.

Jesus Speaks to the Women of Jerusalem

Luke 23:27-28

A great number of the people followed him, and among them were women who were beating their breasts and wailing for him. But Jesus turned to them and said, 'Daughters of Jerusalem, do not weep for me, but weep for yourselves and for your children.'

Psalm 33

The eyes of the Lord are on the righteous
    and his ears are open to their cry....
When the righteous cry for help, the Lord hears
    and rescues them from all their troubles.
The Lord is near to the broken-hearted;
    and saves the crushed in spirit.

Until modern biology taught us about chromosomes, it was believed that the mother contributed nothing to the nature of the child in her womb; she was only a receptacle for the male seed, which was thought to be a little human being, 'homunculus'. Now it is known that the parents contribute equally to the biological make-up of the child.

That older understanding did little to underline the reality of the Incarnation; one wonders how they managed to keep that doctrine in place – and of course some did not. For Mary to be God-bearer, *Theotokos,* is a deeper mystery for us now. The Word took flesh not only *in* Mary but *from* her. And that nature is ours, it is human nature.

The role of all women, and not only Mary's, was lessened by that older understanding (and of course by other factors too). Christian history, even while elevating Mary, has often allowed women only a shadowy reality. 'It is woman's misfortune,' wrote Kierkegaard (1813-1855), 'to represent everything one moment, and to represent nothing the next moment, without ever truly knowing what she properly signifies as a woman.' One moment she is man's esoteric dream, due to evaporate the next moment when he wakes up. At one time serious theologians questioned woman's direct relationship with God. There is a large and very painful literature in this vein.

'The modern, profoundly masculine world, where the feminine charism plays no role whatsoever, is more and more a world without God, for it has no mother and God cannot be born in it,' wrote the Russian theologian Paul Evdokimov. In the Church there will be deeper and deeper dialogue with women; the feminine charisms are needed more than ever. The eighth Station is often called 'Jesus *consoles* the women of Jerusalem.' In the gospel accounts he does something closer to the opposite: he tells them to expect worse than what they are witnessing now. To turn this into 'consoles' – and to keep it that way – required generations of very patronising minds!

Here is a text from Meister Eckhart in which he is speaking about love of God. He interprets the relationship between Adam and Eve in a way that was unconventional then. It is interesting that this is how modern exegesis interprets it now.

> So much should your love be *one,* for love does not wish to be anywhere but where there is likeness and oneness. Where there is a master and servant there is no peace, for there is no likeness. A woman and a man are unlike, but in love they are alike. And so scripture rightly says that God took woman from the man's rib and side and not from the head or from the feet; for where there are two, there is a lack. Why? One 'is not' the other, for the *not* that makes the difference is nothing but bitterness, because there is no peace.

Jesus Falls a Third Time

Romans 15:2-3
Each of us must please our neighbour for the good purpose of building up the neighbour. For Christ did not please himself; but, as it is written, 'The insults of those who insult you have fallen on me.'

Psalm 34
At my stumbling they gathered in glee,
they gathered together against me; …
they tore at me without ceasing:
they impiously mocked more and more
gnashing at me with their teeth.
O Lord, how long will you look on?
Rescue me from their ravages!

✠

Irenaeus of Lyons (A.D. c. 120 or 140 to c. 200 or 203) emphasised the physical reality of Jesus, against the Gnostics who were inclined to downplay or even deny this. He wrote:

> [Jesus came] not despising or evading any condition of humanity … but sanctifying every age …. For he came to

save all: infants and children, boys and girls, young people and old. He therefore passed through every age, becoming an infant for infants, thus sanctifying infants; a child for children, thus sanctifying those of that age … a youth for youths, thus sanctifying them for the Lord. So likewise He was an old man for the old, that He might be a perfect Master for all. … Then, at last, he came to death itself, that He might be 'the first-born from the dead, that in all things He might have the pre-eminence,' the Prince of life, existing before all, and going before all.'

Irenaeus over-stretched his case, claiming that Jesus was in his late 40s at the time of his death. The intention was good: to keep him here long enough to sanctify old age. Still, age is not entirely a matter of numbers; sometimes we are older in our youth than we become later on. Meister Eckhart once said, 'My soul is as young as when she was created, in fact much younger! And I tell you, I should be ashamed if she were not younger tomorrow than today!' Old age is more about *weakness*, and in that sense Jesus experienced old age.

We do not have a high priest who is unable to sympathise with our weaknesses, but we have one who in every respect has been tested as we are, yet without sin …. He is able to deal gently with the ignorant and wayward, since he himself is subject to weakness.

Power is made perfect in weakness. So, I will boast all the more gladly of my weaknesses, so that the power of Christ may dwell in me.

That someone as strong and durable (and proud!) as St Paul could write like this (the last quotation above) is another remarkable piece of evidence that the way of Jesus is able to transform people. He learned to talk even about the *weakness of God*. Simon Tugwell writes:

> There is something about God which is better expressed in weakness than in strength, in foolishness than in wisdom, in poverty than in richness. The story of the earthly life of Jesus Christ is a story of human failure, of human poverty, of human foolishness. And yet that is the revelation of God in human terms. And we who are followers of Jesus Christ are called to be imitators of him, and so should not be at all surprised to find that one of the arts we have to learn is the sublime art of weakness.

Jesus Is Stripped of His Garments

John 19:23-24
When the soldiers had crucified Jesus, they took his clothes and divided them into four parts, one for each soldier. They also took his tunic; now the tunic was seamless, woven in one piece from neck to hem. So they said to one another, 'Let us not tear it, but cast lots to see who will get it.' This was to fulfil what the scripture says, 'They divided my clothes among themselves, and for my clothing they cast lots.'

Luke 2:6-7
While they were there, the time came for her to deliver her child. And she gave birth to her firstborn son and wrapped him in bands of cloth, and laid him in a manger.

✠

We say 'Clothes make the man,' but we also say, 'The habit doesn't make the monk.' I wonder why. A monk is presumed to be searching under the layers of appearances for the essence of humanity, and when he turns back or finds nothing we are very conscious of his failure. We think less about the failure of the other. But today we are more aware than in the past that the search is every man's and woman's search. 'Who am I?' rather than 'How do I want to appear?'

Clothes give you a social identity, they mark you as a member of a class or type. And they also enable you to define a certain individuality within your type: respectable but high-spirited, careless but likeable, and so on …. They have the expressiveness of a language: noun + adjective. Uniforms are an attempt (not a very successful one) to suppress variations on the theme. But naked, you know neither in general nor in particular who you are – unless you have gone deeper than the outer layers. When you are naked you are nobody in particular, you are just a universal human being.

Jesus was stripped of his garments. There was no practical need to do that. They wanted not only to kill but to exterminate him. They thought he would have no remaining identity. But his identity is now indeed 'the Son of Man'. And when he died, even the uniformed pagan soldier would say, 'Truly, this man was the God's Son.'

Many times in his life Jesus had to cast off the false identities that others tried to impose on him. As a child he already knew that he was not just a nice family boy, but that he had to be about his Father's business. Twenty years later people said, 'Is not this the son of Joseph?' Another time they wanted to make him king, but he slipped through their hands and went away. When he asked his closest, 'Who do people say I am?' they answered with a litany of names of dead people. He was none of these things, none of these people. He was a Nobody. But in a rare moment he said, 'The Father and I are one.'

Speaking about spiritual poverty – the *kenosis,* the 'self-empty-ing', like that of Christ – Johann Tauler said:

> There must be nothing left in us but a pure intention toward God; no will to be or become or obtain anything for ourselves. We must exist only to make a place for Him, the highest innermost place, where He may do His work; there, when we are no longer putting ourselves in His way, He can he born in us …. Nothing can be receptive until it is empty and passive and free.

> St Augustine said: 'Empty yourself, so that you may be filled; go out, so that you can go in.' And in another place he said: 'Why do you seek outside yourself for something which in its most constant, truest and purest form is within you? You share God's own nature: what business can you have with created things?'

> If you would prepare an empty place in the depths of his soul there can be no doubt that God must fill it at once. If there were a void on earth the heaven would fall to fill it. God will not allow anything to be void. That would be contrary to His nature and His just ordinance.

> So you must be silent. Then God will be born in you, utter His word in you and you shall hear it; but be very sure that if you speak, the word will have to be silent. The best way to serve the word is to keep silent and listen. If you go out, He will most surely come in; as much as you go out for Him, He will come in to you; no more, no less.

Jesus Is Nailed
to the Cross

Job 17:1-2

'My spirit is broken, my days are extinct, the grave is ready for me. Surely there are mockers around me, and my eye grows dwells on their provocation.'

Luke 23:33

When they came to the place that is called The Skull, they crucified Jesus there with the criminals, one on his right and one on his left.

Matthew 27:37-38

Above his head they put the charge against him, which read, 'This is Jesus, the King of the Jews.' Then two bandits were crucified with him, one on his right and one on his left.

There are many who remind us that suffering is our best teacher, and it is a hard saying. The Christian faith is seldom allowed to challenge the ego; instead it is used to extend it to infinity. But saints are people who have received the challenge and lived by it. They assure us that there is no such thing as a painless life, and therefore running from pain cannot be the

answer: we only run into the arms of greater pain. Yes, they tell
us, exclude all foolish self-imposed pain. Work with what is left
– the inevitable pain of life. Rest at peace with this pain: it is
your best teacher and friend; it opens the gate to life. It
questions your understanding of who and what you are. It takes
away your cushions so that you can feel reality. It does not
follow the contours of your illusions and your strategies for
comfort. This is not horrible, it is a promise of life – because
only reality can save us. If things go against you, the saints tell
us, don't take it as a personal insult; it is God trusting you. The
dream of endless comfort is an insult, not this. God loves you
enough to take you out of yourself.

We usually pray to be rid of suffering, but Julian of Norwich did
the opposite: she prayed to suffer! She asked God for three
things:

> The first was memory of Christ's Passion .... I wanted to be
> actually there at that time with Mary Magdalene, and with
> the others who loved him, and with my own eyes to see and
> know more of the physical suffering of our Saviour, and to
> have compassion for our Lady and for those who there and
> then were loving him truly and watching his pains. I would
> be one of them and suffer with him.

> The second was bodily sickness in youth, at thirty years of
> age .... My intention was that I should be wholly cleansed
> thereby through the mercy of God, and that thereafter,
> because of that illness, I might live more worthily of him.

> The third was to have of God's gift three wounds ....namely,
> the wound of true contrition, the wound of genuine

compassion, and the wound of sincere longing for God.

It is more usual to ask God to heal our wounds. Julian teaches us that there are also wounds that should never be healed, wounds without which we would be less human and less open to grace. To follow the Way of the Cross is to be with Jesus in his suffering. Contrition, compassion and longing for God are wounds that should remain open forever. To refuse these wounds is to refuse to love. The cross of Christ challenges every project of self-fulfilment, every definition of who we are and what our life means.

In his *Little Book of Eternal Wisdom,* written in dialogue form, Henry Suso says:

> If you have no inclination to meditate on my Passion with weeping, then meditate on it with a laughing heart, because of its great benefits to you. But if you have no mind either to laugh or to cry, then meditate on it in the dryness of your heart. You will derive no less benefit this way, for you are acting from love of virtue, without self-regard.

Jesus Dies on the Cross

Luke 23:34
Then Jesus said, 'Father, forgive them, for they do not know what they are doing.'

Mark 15:33-37
When it was noon, darkness came over the whole land until three in the afternoon. At three o'clock Jesus cried out with a loud voice, 'Eloi, Eloi, lema sabachthani?' which means, 'My God, my God, why have you forsaken me?' When some of the bystanders heard it they said, 'Listen, he is calling for Elijah.' And someone ran, filled a sponge with sour wine, put it on a stick, and gave it to him to drink, saying, 'Wait, let us see whether Elijah will come to take him down.' Then Jesus gave a loud cry and breathed his last.

Romans 5:8-10
God proves his love for us is that while we were still sinners Christ died for us. Much more surely then, now that we have been justified by his blood, will we be saved through him from the wrath of God. For if while we were enemies, we were reconciled to God through the death of his Son, much more surely, having been reconciled, will we be saved by his life.

✠

'Self-knowledge is impossible for you in the West,' said an Indian teacher some years ago, 'because you are unwilling to pass through suffering.' You are not looking for wisdom, he said, you are looking for tranquillisers. You say you are looking for ways of meditation, but you are only looking for new ways of drugging yourselves. Meditation is bound to pass through suffering. It is not a pastime.

It is strange that the Western world, which has been so profoundly shaped by the Christian faith, should have to be reminded of this by someone who was not a Christian. The story of Christ's suffering lies deep in the spirit of anyone who has ever been touched by the Christian faith. Its image, the cross, is visible everywhere.

'People who have not suffered, what do they know?' said Henry Suso, a man who suffered more than most in a century (the fourteenth) that suffered more than most. Here is his statement in context:

> There is nothing more painful than suffering, and nothing more joyful than to have suffered. Suffering is short pain and long joy. Suffering has this effect on the one to whom suffering is suffering, that it ceases to be suffering …. Suffering makes a wise and practised person. People who have not suffered, what do they know … ? All the saints are the cup-bearers of a suffering person, for they have all tasted it once themselves, and they cry out with one voice that it is free from poison and a wholesome drink.

'The one to whom suffering is suffering.' He is being precise about this. To many who suffer, suffering isn't suffering as such, but anguish and misery and rejection of suffering. The word 'to suffer' in English means 'to allow', whereas the word 'anguish' comes from the Latin 'ang(u)ere', which means 'to choke'. Suffering, Suso persuades us, is 'a wholesome drink.' We should not choke on it. The saints have tasted it before handing us the cup; they are the proof that it is not poison.

God's mercy did not protect Jesus from suffering, nor Mary, nor any of his disciples through the ages. We cannot expect that it will protect us. It would be protecting us from life, and that would be no mercy.

This 'knowledge' of the meaning of suffering is not book-knowledge or factual knowledge; it is *experience* that continues day by day and is never finished. It is not the kind of knowledge that gives us security and control: these often serve only to close the heart. It is first-hand knowledge – the only kind that is able to open us to new life.

We are not alone in our suffering. 'The Passion of Christ belongs to us as fully as if we had suffered it ourselves,' wrote St Thomas Aquinas. This is a statement of extraordinary depth and power. It means that we do not cower before the Father in guilt and shame; instead we stand before the Father in the person of Jesus, the Beloved Son. The Father can see no difference between us and Jesus. Julian of Norwich wrote:

> In his great and everlasting love for all humankind, God makes no distinction between the holy soul of Christ, and

the most insignificant soul to be saved. It is very easy to believe and trust that the holy soul of Christ has a supreme place of honour in the glorious Godhead; yet if I truly understand our Lord's meaning, where Christ's blessed soul is, there too, in their essential being, are all the souls who are going to be saved by him.

Jesus Is Taken Down from the Cross

Mark 15:42-46

When evening had come, and since it was the day of Preparation, that is, the day before the sabbath, Joseph of Arimathea, a respected member of the council, who was also himself waiting expectantly for the kingdom of God, went boldly to Pilate and asked for the body of Jesus. Then Pilate wondered if he were already dead; and summoning the centurion, he asked him whether he had been dead for some time. When he learned from the centurion that he was dead, he granted the body to Joseph. Then Joseph bought a linen cloth, and taking down the body, wrapped it in the linen cloth, and laid it in a tomb that had been hewn out of the rock. He then rolled a stone against the door to the tomb.

John 19: 25-27

Standing near the cross of Jesus were his mother, and his mother's sister, Mary the wife of Clopas, and Mary Magdalene. When Jesus saw his mother and the disciple whom he loved standing beside her, he said to his mother, 'Woman, here is your son.' Then he said to the disciple, 'Here is your mother.' And from that hour the disciple took her into his own home.

1 John 4:9-10

God's love was revealed among us in this way: God sent his only Son into the world so that we might live through him. In this is love, not that we loved God but that God loved us and sent his Son to be the atoning sacrifice for our sins.

The eyes that looked with compassion are staring empty in death, the mouth that spoke as no one spoke is silent. The deed is done and evil has had its way. 'Blessed are the meek,' he had said, 'for they shall inherit the earth.' His dead body seems the falsification of all the Beatitudes. It represents what the world does to the poor in spirit, to those who mourn, who are meek, who hunger and thirst for what is right, who are merciful, pure in heart, peacemakers, and to all who have been persecuted and reviled throughout the ages. The promises made to them seem hollow now: that they will inherit not only the earth but the kingdom of God, that they will receive mercy, and see God.

Peace is obtained only by victory, said Cicero, offering the best wisdom that an ancient Roman could offer. There is also a kind of peace in defeat, when the worst has happened. These two kinds of peace the world can give and always gives. There is a third kind: a beautiful romanticised peace, childlike in its innocence, but older than the new age. Mediaeval Irish monks were not insensible to it, but because of their hard lives they were perhaps more entitled to it than we today. It is the song of the once-born. Here it is in a twelfth-century poem, *St Columba's*

Delightful I think it to be in the bosom of an isle, on the peak of a rock, that I might often see there the calm of the sea.

That I might see its heavy waves over the glittering ocean, as they chant a melody to their Father on their eternal course.

That I might see its smooth strand of clear headlands, no gloomy thing; that I might hear the voice of the wondrous birds, a joyful tune.

That I might hear the sound of the shallow waves against the rocks; that I might hear the cry by the graveyard, the noise of the sea.

That I might see its splendid flocks of birds over the full-watered ocean; that I might see its mighty whales, greatest of wonders ….

That I might pore on one of my books, good for my soul; a while kneeling for beloved Heaven, a while at psalms.

A while gathering dulse from the rock, a while fishing, a while giving food to the poor, a while in my cell.

A while meditating upon the Kingdom of Heaven, holy is the redemption; a while at labour not too heavy; it would be delightful!

There were similar poems of longing in the previous centuries, somewhat more austere. These lovely dreams of peace, however, could be (and were) destroyed in the plundering raids of the Vikings. What is the peace that Christ promised? The

Vikings have come, every 'secret hermitage' and 'remote hidden little hut' – dreams perhaps of the self – is laid in ruins. We have to sit without words or dreams by the dead body of Jesus and know death to the bone. We may be called beyond self-indulgent fantasies to a place where we know nothing but pity. The Church is to be the *Pietà*, grieving like a mother for her children.

There are many lesser beatitudes that the world can give. But dying to the self, taking up one's cross and following to the end: that is what opens our lives to the real Beatitudes.

Jesus Is Laid in the Tomb

Matthew 27:59,60
Joseph took the body and wrapped it in a clean linen cloth and laid it in his own new tomb, which he had hewn in the rock. He then rolled a great stone to the door of the tomb and went away.

Luke 23:54-56
It was the day of Preparation, and the sabbath was beginning. The women who had come with him from Galilee followed, and they saw the tomb and how his body was laid. Then they returned and prepared spices and ointments. And on the sabbath they rested according to the commandment.

Romans 6:3-4
Do you not know that all of us who have been baptised into Christ Jesus were baptised into his death? Therefore we have been buried with him by baptism into death, so that, just as Christ was raised from the dead by the glory of the Father, so we too might walk in newness of life.

Jesus not only tasted death, he was swallowed up in it; he went 'down into' the tomb. The Eucharist is not celebrated on Holy

Saturday. The altars are stripped bare, tabernacles lie open and empty. The whole Church is one with him in his death. We do not jump suddenly from Friday to Sunday. Death is given time and space to be itself in all its helplessness.

On Holy Saturday the Church contemplates the mystery of the Lord's descent into 'Hades' or 'Sheol', the place of the dead. Death, the final enemy, has to be defeated from within. It is ironic that Jesus, who was so often accused of breaking the Law by working on the sabbath, should still be breaking it after his death! He 'descended into hell,' as the Apostles' Creed says, and liberated from that place of shadows all the just who had died since Adam. It was the 'place' where everyone went after death; it was not a place of punishment, but was pictured as a land of shadows and forgetfulness: God had forgotten all who lived their dismal afterlife there, and they had forgotten God. In the apocryphal writings of the early centuries there are several accounts of the arrival of Jesus in that bleak underworld.

> When we were placed with our fathers in the depth of Sheol, in the black darkness, all of a sudden there appeared the colour of the sun like gold …. Adam, the father of the human race, with all the patriarchs and prophets, rejoiced …. Then David said to the prince of hell, 'Open the gates, that the King of Glory may enter in; for he is the Lord of heaven and earth.' While David was saying this, the mighty Lord appeared, and filled with light those places which had always been in darkness. He broke asunder the fetters which before could not be broken; and with his invincible power visited those who sat in darkness and in the shadow of death.

In another account, one of the people who was being liberated into the light of the Resurrection said to Jesus, 'Plant here in the pit of hell your Cross, so that there will forever be hope for all who pass this way.' And in the pit of hell Jesus planted his cross, now no longer a symbol of death and shame but a symbol of hope and new life.

The 'Descent among the Dead' was a favourite theme of Christian artists through the middle ages until it was gradually eclipsed. Nowadays it seems to be slowly returning. It is a theme that has rich associations. Everyone has a personal Sheol: the past, all the forgotten days and nights of one's life. There are many things in one's life that need to be brought out into the light of the resurrection. Likewise every group and every country has its Sheol, awaiting the arrival of the Lord of Life. The Jewish scholar George Steiner wrote that our world today is a kind of prolonged Holy Saturday: the age between Friday and Sunday, between defeat and hope. He was thinking, no doubt, about Auschwitz, Hiroshima, Chernobyl ….

Everyone today, Steiner says – Jews, Christians and atheists – knows Good Friday in one way or another: the day of 'interminable suffering, of waste, of the brute enigma of ending … the pain, the failure of love, the solitude which are our history and private fate.' And we also know Easter Sunday in some way: 'the day of resurrection, of a justice and a love that have conquered death.' But then he speaks of Saturday, 'the longest of days … between suffering, aloneness, unutterable waste on the one hand and the dream of liberation, of rebirth on the other.'

We have to sit by the tomb of the dead Christ and give death time to be itself. Only by living through Holy Saturday have we the right to hope for Easter Sunday.

Jesus Is Raised from the Dead

John 20:11-18

Mary stood weeping outside the tomb. As she wept, she bent over to look into the tomb; and she saw two angels in white, sitting where the body of Jesus had been lying, one at the head and the other at the feet. They said to her, 'Woman, why are you weeping?' She said to them, 'They have taken away my Lord, and I do not know where they have laid him.' When she had said this she turned around and saw Jesus standing there, but she did not know that it was Jesus. Jesus said to her, 'Woman, why are you weeping? Whom are you seeking?' Supposing him to be the gardener, she said to him, 'Sir, if you have carried him away, tell me where you have laid him, and I will take him away.' Jesus said to her, 'Mary!' She turned and said to him in Hebrew, 'Rabbuni!' (which means Teacher). Jesus said to her, 'Do not hold on to me, because I have not yet ascended to the Father. But go to my brothers and say to them, 'I am ascending to my Father and your Father, to my God and your God.' Mary Magdalene went and announced to the disciples, 'I have seen the Lord'; and she told them that he had said these things to her.

1 Corinthians 15:12-17

If Christ is proclaimed as raised from the dead, how can some of you say there is no resurrection of the dead? If there is no resurrection of the dead, then Christ has not been raised; and if Christ has not been raised, then our proclamation has been in vain and your faith has been in vain. We are even found to be misrepresenting God, because we testified of God that he raised Christ – whom he did not raise if it is true that the dead are not raised. If Christ has not been raised, your faith is futile and you are still in your sins.'

It is Easter Sunday that makes Good Friday good. It is the end that gives meaning to a story. Through the centuries millions of people have survived terrible Calvaries because they had learnt something utterly profound from the Cross of Christ. That he died *and was buried* underlines the *newness* of the new life of the resurrection.

The following is from an ancient homily for Holy Saturday:

> I command you: Awake, sleeper, I have not made you to be held a prisoner in the underworld. Arise from the dead; I am the life of the dead. Arise, O human being, work of my hands, arise, you who were fashioned in my image. Rise, let us go hence; for you in me and I in you, together we are one undivided person …. Arise, let us go hence. The enemy brought you out of the land of paradise; I will reinstate you, no longer in paradise, but on the throne of heaven. I denied you the tree of life, which was an image, but now I myself am united to you, I who am life.

In the darkness we rise for the Easter Vigil. Against a black sky we light the Easter fire. But this would be a forlorn gesture if Christ were not risen from the dead! Suddenly the Paschal candle is alight. *Lumen Christi!* – the light of Christ lightens our darkness. *Exsultet!* – 'Exult, all creation … !'

> Rejoice, heavenly powers! Sing, choirs of angels!
>> Exult, all creation around God's throne!
>> Jesus Christ, our King, is risen!
>> Sound the trumpet of salvation!

> Rejoice, O earth, shining splendour,
>> radiant in the brightness of your King!
>> Christ has conquered! Glory fills you!
>> Darkness vanishes for ever!

> Rejoice, O Mother Church! Exult in glory!
>> The risen Saviour shines upon you!
>> Let this place resound with joy,
>> echoing the mighty song of all God's people … !

> This is the night when Christians everywhere,
>> washed clean of sin
>> and freed from all defilement,
>> are restored to grace and grow together in holiness.

> This is the night when Jesus Christ
>> broke the chains of death
>> and rose triumphant from the grave.

> What good would life have been to us,
>> had Christ not come as our Redeemer?
> Father, how wonderful your care for us!

How boundless your merciful love!
To ransom a slave you gave away your Son.

O happy fault, O necessary sin of Adam
which gained for us so great a Redeemer!

Most blessed of nights, chosen by God
to see Christ rising from the dead!

Of this night scripture says:
'The night will be as clear as the day:
it will become my light, my joy!' …

May the morning Star which never sets find this flame still
burning:
Christ, that Morning Star, who came back from the
dead,
and shed his peaceful light on all humankind,
your Son who lives and reigns for ever and ever.
Amen.

It is not a time for looking at ourselves and trying to sort ourselves out; it is not a time for raking through the ashes of our dead hopes; it is not even a time for self-improvement. Instead it is a time to look up at the slopes where the sun is rising!

Angels, roll the rock away;
Death, yield up thy mighty prey:
See, He rises from the tomb,
Glowing with immortal bloom.
Alleluia! Alleluia!
Christ the Lord is risen today!'

References

Introduction
Job 18:14
2 Corinthians 5:14
2 Timothy 2:11
Luke 24:32

Prayer before the Stations
Douglas Hyde

The Way of the Cross
First Station
Lamentations 1:1
T.S. Eliot, *The Hollow Men* (1925)

Second Station
Mark 10:32
Isaiah 53:7; Acts 8:32

Third Station
Hebrews 4:15

Fourth Station
Dante, *Divina Commedia,* 'Paradiso'.

Sixth Station
Luke 23:27
Julian of Norwich, *Shewings,* chapter 51
William Wordsworth, 'Lines Composed a Few Miles above Tintern
Abbey' (1798).

Seventh Station
Hebrews 1:3
2 Peter 1:19
1 Peter 2:24

Ninth Station
John 5:11
Matthew 25:40

Tenth Station
Luke 9:58
Julian of Norwich, *Shewings,* chapter 51
Colossians 1:15
Luke 12:15
Luke 12:33
Matthew 5:3
Mark 1:11

Eleventh Station
Matthew 12:13
John 5:8
John 12:47
John 10:10
Luke 23:34
1 Corinthians 2:8

Thirteenth Station
John 12:24
The word 'humility' is derived from the Latin '*humus*', meaning 'earth'. 'Blessed Earth, blissful spouse of God….'
Johann Tauler, *Spiritual Conferences* (trans. and ed. by Eric Colledge and Sr M. Jane), Sermon 1 for the Nativity.
John 13:1

Fourteenth Station
1 Corinthians 15:3
1 Thessalonians 4:13

Fifteenth Station
From the Liturgy of the Easter Vigil

Resources
First Station
Matthew 7:1
The Divine Names, chapter 3.
Sermon 131

Second Station
Mark 10:32
'Our paschal lamb, Christ, has been sacrificed' (1 Corinthians 5:7).

Third Station

> *Shewings,* chapter 51: 'He seid not "Thou shalt not be tempestid,
> thou shalt not be travelled [in travail], thou shalt not be disesid
> [without ease]", but he seid: "Thou shalt not be overcome." '

Fourth Station

> Psalm 33:9. See Colossians 1:14 'All things were created through
> him [the Word] and for him. He is before all things, and in him
> all things hold together.'
> *Letter to the Ephesians*, n. 15

Fifth Station

> Job 7:1-2
> *Commentary on the Book of Job*, Book 10
> *Little Book of Truth*, chapter 7
> *Meister Eckhart: Sermons and Treatises*, trans. and ed., M. O'C.
> Walshe, vol. 1, sermon 13

Sixth Station

> *Shewings,* chapter 51
> *Gitanjali*, n. 43

Seventh Station

> Matthew 12:10; Mark 3:3; Luke 6:8
> John 5:2-9
> Luke 14:21
> *Mathnawi*, VI

Eighth Station

> 'The Seducer'.
> *Woman and the Salvation of the World.*
> *Meister Eckhart: Sermons and Treatises*, vol. 1, sermon 1261

Ninth Station

> *Adversus Haereses*, Bk 1, ch. 22
> *op. cit.,* vol. 2, sermon 80
> Hebrews 4:15; 5:2
> 2 Corinthians 12:9
> 1 Corinthians 1:25
> *Reflections on the Beatitudes,* Introduction

Tenth Station
  Matthew 27:54
  Luke 2:49
  John 6:42
  John 6:15
  Matthew 16:14
  John 10:30
  Spiritual Conferences, Sermon 1 for the Nativity.

Eleventh Station
  Shewings, chapter 2
  chapter 14

Twelfth Station
  Chapter 13
  Summa Theologiae, III q. 69, a.2
  Shewings, ch. 54

Thirteenth Station
  Matthew 5:5

Fourteenth Station
  Psalm 6:5 'In death there is no remembrance of You; in Sheol who
    can give you praise?'
  The Acts of Pilate, chapters 13, 16
  Real Presences, in fine

Fifteenth Station
  Liturgy of the Easter Vigil, 'The Easter Proclamation (*Exsultet*)'
  Thomas Scott, *Easter Angels*